EDITOR: Jenny Corsey GRAPHIC DESIGN: Cecil Anderson and Lynette Rowe COVER DESIGN: Victoria DeJoy

CAROLE MARSH BOOKS

Published by
GALLOPADE™ INTERNATIONAL
800-536-2GET
www.gallopade.com

Gallopade is proud to be a member of these educational organizations and associations:

The National School Supply and Equipment Association
The National Council for the Social Studies
Association for Supervision and Curriculum Development
Museum Store Association
Association of Partners for Public Lands

Other Carole Marsh Holiday Books

Kwanzaa Activities, Crafts, Recipes, and More!
Hanukkah Activities, Crafts, Recipes, and More!

Holiday Readers™ Series
The Story of Santa Claus
The Story of the Christmas Tree
The Legend of the Candy Cane
Why Do We Hang Christmas Stockings?
Christmas Traditions Around the World
Christmas Recipes From the Past

New Traditions™ Series
The Victorian Crazy Christmas Cobweb Party Kit
The Secret Christmas Potpourri & Tussie Mussie Story Kit
The Epiphany Surprise Christmas Cake Story Kit
The Chinese Fortune Cookie Christmas Story & Ornament Kit

State Christmas Trivia™ (all 50 states available!)

The Penguin Strut Fashion Show
The Snow Bank
Winter The "Wow!" Season
A Carolina Christmas
The Cowboys' Christmas Ball

A Word From the Author

Dear Readers

Snowflakes on my eyelashes, steaming hot chocolate, carolers at the door, the scents of peppermint and pine wafting throughout the house... these are some of my favorite sights, sounds, smells, and tastes of Christmas. And it's all coming very soon!

This book is packed with wonderful stories, interesting facts, great crafts, and lots more for you to enjoy during the Christmas season (*or* anytime you just WANT it to be Christmas!). I've included games, songs, puzzles, trivia, poems, projects, recipes, and lots more–even a family Christmas newsletter. Don't hesitate to add to the fun! Remember, when it comes to celebrating Christmas with your loved ones, a truly creative mind can always come up with endless ideas!

This special season is celebrated all around the world from Australia to Greenland. So whether you are building a snowman or a sandcastle this December, I hope this activity book will help you learn more about this special holiday.

Merry Christmas!

Carole Marsh & the Gallopade Gang

Carole Marsh

The History of Christmas

Ancient Days

People in the Northern Hemisphere try to awaken the sun god every December by singing and dancing around a huge bonfire, fueled by a great "Yule" log.

Romans honor Saturnus (the harvest god) and Mithras (the ancient god of light) during Saturnalia, which is observed between December 17 and 24,.

274 AD

Solstice falls on December 25. Roman Emperor Aurelian decrees the "Natalis Solis Invicti" festival on that day to celebrate the birth of the invincible sun.

320 AD

Pope Julius declares that December 25 is the official birth date of Jesus Christ, even though He was born in March. People had been observing the famous birth on many wrong dates for more than 300 years!

325 AD

Constantine the Great, the first Christian Roman emperor, decides everyone should celebrate the birth of Jesus Christ and enacts a Christmas feast day on December 25. Christians refuse to celebrate on the day of a pagan holiday.

354 AD

Bishop Liberius of Rome requires all church members to celebrate the birth of Jesus Christ on December 25.

1649-1660

Oliver Cromwell of England forbids Christmas festivities because he thinks it should be observed as a reverent and dignified day.

1820

Washington Irving writes a book called *The Keeping of Christmas at Bracebridge Hall,* which inspires more people to celebrate the holiday.

1834

Charles Dickens publishes *A Christmas Carol* a week before Christmas.

1836

Alabama is the first state in the U.S. to declare Christmas a legal holiday.

1860

Famous American illustrator Thomas Nast creates a Father Christmas character after the old European stories about Saint Nicholas.

Celebrate the Joy of Christmas!

Circle the things you might enjoy on this joyous holiday! Color the pictures.

Crack the Christmas Code!

Use the code to discover some traditional holiday expressions!

A	B	C	D	E	F	G	H	I	J	K	L	M
✹	❀	✣	♣	➳	❤	❢	✲	✄	✆	☛	✈	✉

N	O	P	Q	R	S	T	U	V	W	X	Y	Z
❦	☎	✒	✚	✖	✍	✠	✓	✿	✰	✦	✡	✐

1. ___ ___ ___ ___ ___   ___ ___ ___ ___ ___ ___ ___ ___ ___!
   ✉ ➳ ✖ ✖ ✡   ✣ ✲ ✖ ✄ ✍ ✠ ✉ ✹ ✍

2. ___ ___ ___ ___   ___ ___ ___   ___ ___ ___ ___ ___!
   ♣ ➳ ✣ ☛   ✠ ✲ ➳   ✲ ✹ ✈ ✈ ✍

3. ___ ___ ___ ___ ___   ___ ___
   ✒ ➳ ✹ ✣ ➳   ❀ ➳

   ___ ___ ___ ___   ___ ___ ___!
   ✰ ✄ ✠ ✲   ✡ ☎ ✓

4. ___ ___ ___ ___ ___   ___ ___ ___ ___ ___ ___ ___ ___!
   ✲ ✹ ✒ ✒ ✡   ✲ ☎ ✈ ✄ ♣ ✹ ✡ ✍

5. ___ ___ ___   ___ ___   ___ ___ ___   ___ ___ ___ ___ ___!
   ✆ ☎ ✡   ✠ ☎   ✠ ✲ ➳   ✰ ☎ ✖ ✈ ♣

ANSWER KEY: Merry Christmas, Deck the Halls, Peace Be With You, Happy Holidays, Joy to the World

Read All About It!

Dear Reader,

Does your family send a Christmas newsletter to relatives and friends each year? If not, perhaps you can begin a new tradition in your home! Write the names of each family member on index cards. Ask everyone to think about what has happened in your household this past year.

Did anyone in your family go on a vacation, graduate from high school, get married, earn a college scholarship, buy a car, score a goal, lose a tooth, win a competition, break an arm, get a job, plant a garden, lose weight, take care of a pet, get braces off, celebrate an anniversary, or get an "A" grade in school?

Make sure everyone fills in lots of "news" from this year on their card. Write a paragraph for each person in your family with the information that they provide. Add an introduction and a conclusion. Lastly, ask someone to proofread your newsletter.

Print the newsletters in a fancy font on pretty Christmas paper. Use colored pens, stickers, and Christmas stamps to address the envelopes. Be sure that every family member signs the newsletter!

Sincerely,

Carole Marsh and the Gallopade Gang

P.S. Merry Christmas!

Stuff Your Own Stocking

Cut out the pattern below. Trace two stockings on red paper. Cut them out. Staple or glue the outside edges together to form a stocking. You could also punch holes along the edge and tie them together with yarn or ribbon bows. Glue cotton balls to fill the top space. Draw or paste pictures of things you might like to have in your stocking this Christmas!

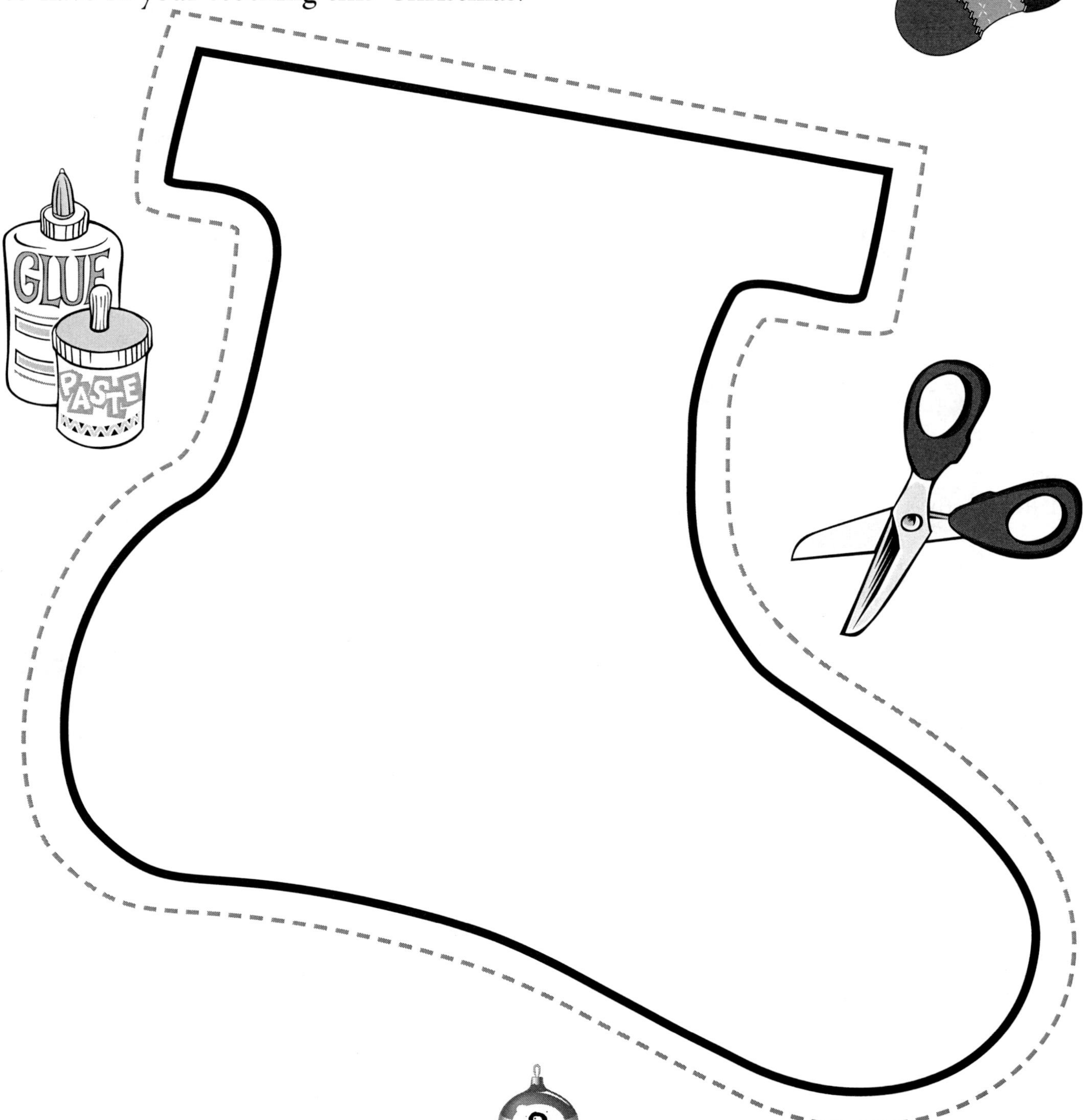

Follow That Nose!

On a cold December evening in 1938, a man named Robert L. May told his daughter Barbara a very special story. They both needed a little cheer because Mrs. May lay in bed, sick with cancer. Her medication cost a lot, so there was no money left for gifts.

Robert set Barbara on his lap and told her about a little reindeer named Rudolph who had a big red nose. He did not like his nose because everyone teased him about it. Then Santa Claus desperately needed him on Christmas Eve. Rudolph's nose lit a path through the fog that night so Santa's sleigh could travel safely to every house!

Barbara *loved* the story and asked her daddy to tell it *every* night! Robert decided to write a poem about Rudolph and make her a book, complete with illustrations, for a Christmas gift. The story helped Robert and Barbara feel a little better when Mrs. May died.

Robert worked for Montgomery Ward, a department store in Chicago. He read his poem during an office Christmas party. People loved it almost as much as Barbara! By 1946, more than 6 million copies had been distributed. Robert's friend Johnny Marks set the poem to music, and cowboy singer Gene Autry recorded the song. Since then, more than 80 million records of "Rudolph the Red-Nosed Reindeer" have been sold. Rudolph is now a legendary Christmas icon!

Write T for true statements and F for false statements.

_____ Rudolph was a blue-nosed reindeer.

_____ Robert L. May worked for a Montgomery Ward store.

_____ Barbara received a homemade book for Christmas in 1938.

_____ Mrs. May was sick with diphtheria.

_____ Robert read his poem for his co-workers at a party.

_____ When the poem was set to music, the record sold more than 70 million copies!

ANSWER KEY: F, T, F, F, T, F

The Greatest Gift

Which month of the year do you begin to compose your Christmas wish list? November? October? January?!? Everyone loves to receive brightly wrapped gifts during the holiday season, but the greatest gift often lies somewhere other than under the tree.

Instead of adding pages to your own wish list, this year write a list of gifts that you plan to *give* to others. Include folks you care about very much, such as your parents, brothers, sisters, grandparents, neighbors, friends, teachers, babysitter, coach, or even your pets. Remember that the you don't necessarily need to go shopping to complete your giving list!

Scan the list of ideas. Write some of your own ideas on another piece of paper!

- Offer to help your mom with the dishes after Christmas dinner.
- Bake some yummy Christmas cookies with an adult, then fill some festive tins for your neighbors!
- Write a special poem for your grandma.
- Design homemade cards for your friends, and tape a small candy cane on the back for a seal.
- Give your dad a book coupons that entitle him to "three hours of yard work," "one grass-cutting," "five car washes," and other chores – all from you!
- Help your babysitter tidy up the house at the end of the night.
- Draw a picture of your extended family and give it to your grandpa.
- Spend some extra time with your pet during Christmas week so he or she won't feel lonely and left out of all the hustle and bustle.
- Make beautiful wrapping paper with colored stamps to cover candy bars as gifts for your siblings. Get their favorites!
- Clean up the equipment with your coach after practice.
- Give your teacher a list of 10 important lessons you have learned from him or her during the school year.

Christmas Around the World!

_______ 1. Families decorate mango and banana trees for Christmas.

_______ 2. Santa arrives to this place on the Christmas Tree Ship each year.

_______ 3. Puppets act out the Christmas story in elaborate plays.

_______ 4. Families burn a Yule log through the twelve days of Christmas.

_______ 5. Children write letters to Father Christmas.

Match each tradition with the correct location.

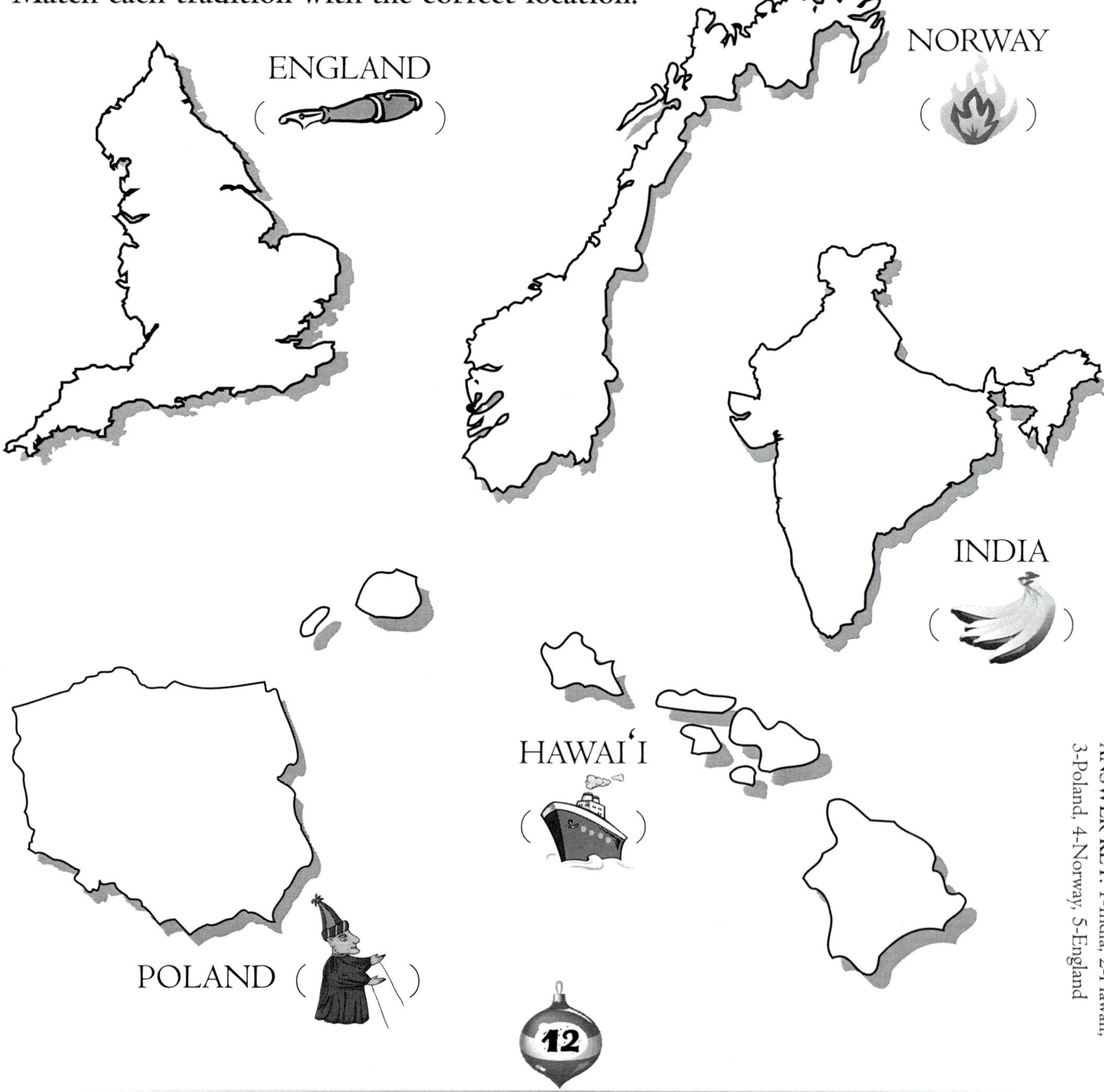

ANSWER KEY: 1-India, 2-Hawaii, 3-Poland, 4-Norway, 5-England

Lift Your Voices!

Fill in the missing letters to complete the Christmas songs. Sing these treasured tunes with your family around the tree some December evening!

"__oy to __he Worl__"

"R__dolph, __he Red-__osed Rein__eer"

"C__estnuts Roastin__ on __n Op__n __ire"

"O C__me __ll Y__ Fait__ful"

"Li__tle Dru__mer __oy"

"__he T__elve Day__ of Ch__istmas"

"Away i__ a M__nger"

"O Christ__as Tr__e"

ANSWER KEY: Joy to the World; Rudolph, the Red-Nosed Reindeer; Chestnuts Roasting on an Open Fire; O Come All Ye Faithful; Little Drummer Boy; The Twelve Days of Christmas; Away in a Manger; O Christmas Tree

Starry Nights

Follow the directions below to fold a five-pointed star. Make several stars. Cover them lightly with glue and set on a sheet of newspaper. Gently scatter glitter across the glue and wait for it to dry. Punch a tiny hole in the top of a point. Thread a skinny silver ribbon through the hole and tie a knot. Hang your Christmas stars on your tree or around the house for a sparkling decoration!

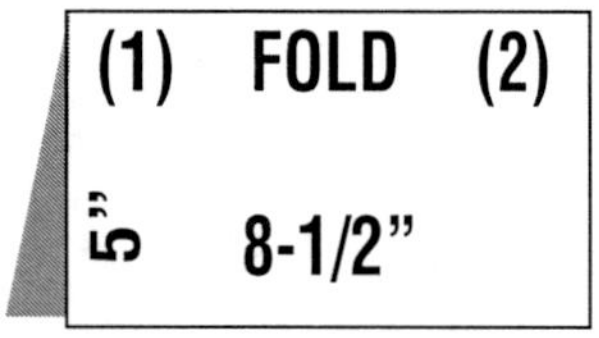

STEP 1

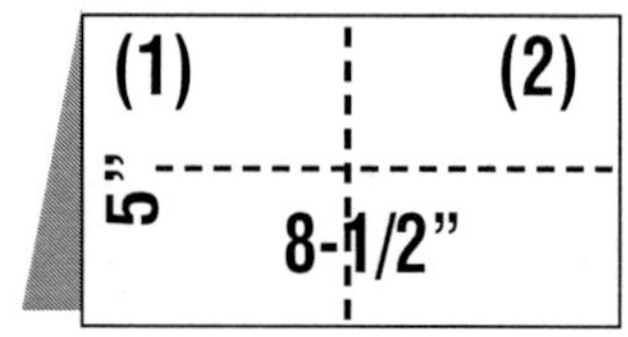

Fold an 8-1/2-by-10-inch piece of paper in half. Leave it folded and then fold it in half from top to bottom and again from side to side. When you unfold it, you should see a cross.

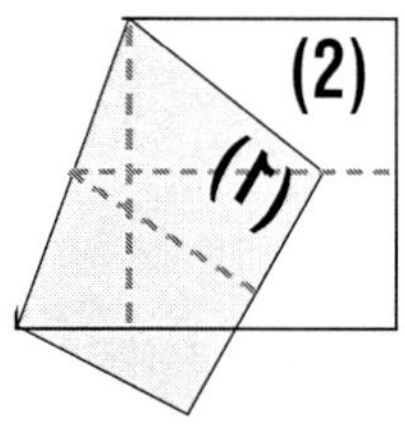

STEP 2

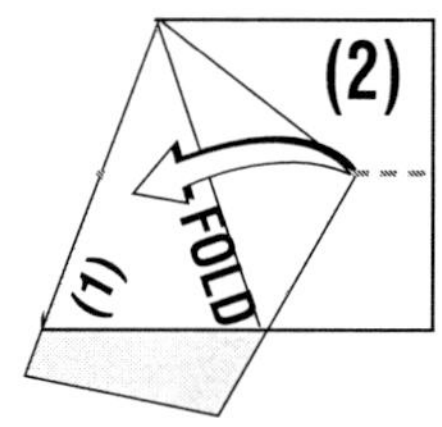

Take the upper left corner (1) and fold it from the center of the top to the crease on the horizontal line. Now take corner 1 and fold it back to the left until it lines up with the left side.

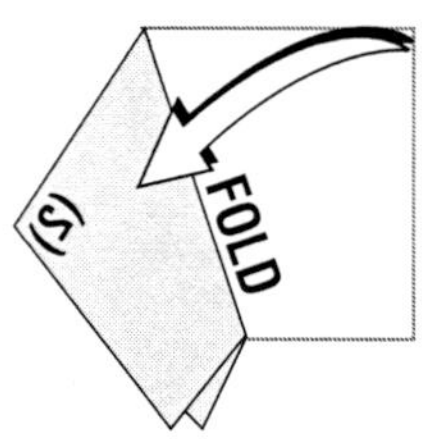

STEP 3

Take the top right corner (2) and fold it over to the left. Then bring corner 2 back to the right and fold it again. The paper now looks a little like a necktie.

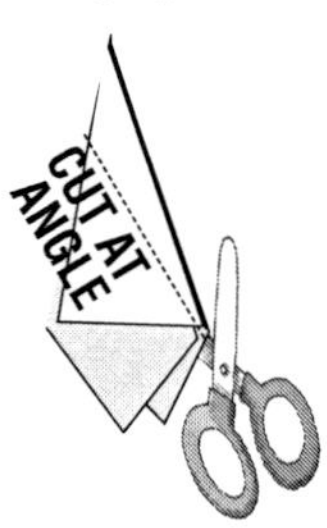

STEP 4

Make a cut from corner 2 across the paper to a point about 1 inch down from the top point. When you unfold this snippet, it should be a perfect five-pointed star!

Chop Down The Tree!

Did you know that…

- Christmas trees are grown in all 50 states, including Hawaii and Alaska?
- Christmas tree farms provide a natural habitat for wildlife?
- More than 98% of Christmas trees are grown on farms?
- Christmas trees remove dust and pollen from the air?
- More than 100,000 people are employed in the Christmas tree industry?
- There are more than 15,000 Christmas tree growers in North America?

Help this family get their Christmas tree home from the tree farm in time for Christmas Eve!

The Legend of the Poinsettia Flower

Long ago, there lived a poor young girl in the country of Mexico. Each year, her church held a Christmas Eve service. People from miles around would come to place gifts by the nativity scene for the Christ Child. The little girl was very sad because she had no gift for the baby.

She sat on the ground outside the church, ashamed to go inside. People bustled past without paying any attention to her. Then someone stopped and looked at her. The stranger, perhaps an angel, whispered something quietly to the little girl. Her face lit up! She gathered some green weeds and brought them inside to lay by the manger. All of a sudden, the weeds turned into brilliant red blooms to create the first poinsettia flower.

According to the legend, the stranger told the little girl that even a very humble gift can be of high worth, if it is given with love. Ever since that Christmas miracle long ago, the green leaves of the poinsettia flower turn crimson red every Christmas season as an everlasting gift.

Read the story. Circle all the nouns. Underline all the verbs.

Send Me...

Every holiday season the United States Postal Service releases a new Christmas postage stamp. The very first postage stamp for Christmas was issued in 1937 in Austria. The first official U.S. Christmas stamp was released in 1962. An artist named Ellen H. Clapsaddle designed themes for these Christmas stamps. Many people like to collect these new stamps each year.

Design your own Christmas postage stamp for this year.

Fast Fact!

Stamp collecting is called philately, two Greek words that mean "the love of tax-free things."

The Twelve Days of Christmas

Give someone a really unique gift this year! Gather inexpensive gifts for each of the 12 days before Christmas Day. Some examples are one chocolate bar, two mittens, three scented soaps, four special photos, five candy canes, etc.

List your gift ideas below, then find a special friend to receive them!

1. ____________________
2. ____________________
3. ____________________
4. ____________________
5. ____________________
6. ____________________
7. ____________________
8. ____________________
9. ____________________
10. ____________________
11. ____________________
12. ____________________

Christmas Sugar Cookies

There are dozens, maybe hundreds of different types of Christmas cookies. How could anyone choose which ones to make for a holiday season? This recipe is a lot of fun because you get to decorate the cookies! Bake away!

Sugar Cookies

Ingredients:

1 1/2 cups powdered sugar
1 cup shortening
1 egg
1 teaspoon vanilla extract
1/2 teaspoon almond extract
2 1/2 cups all-purpose flour
1 teaspoon baking soda
1 teaspoon cream of tartar

To prepare:

1. Mix together sugar, shortening, egg, vanilla extract, and almond extract until creamy.
2. Gradually add flour, baking soda, and cream of tartar. Mix well.
3. Roll out dough to about 1/8" thickness and cut into Christmas shapes with well floured cookie cutters.
4. Place cookies onto lightly greased cookie sheets and decorate with sprinkles, candies, and/or nuts.
5. Bake cookies at 350°F for 8-10 minutes. Allow to cool.
6. Serve warm with a glass of milk!

Cinnamon Children!

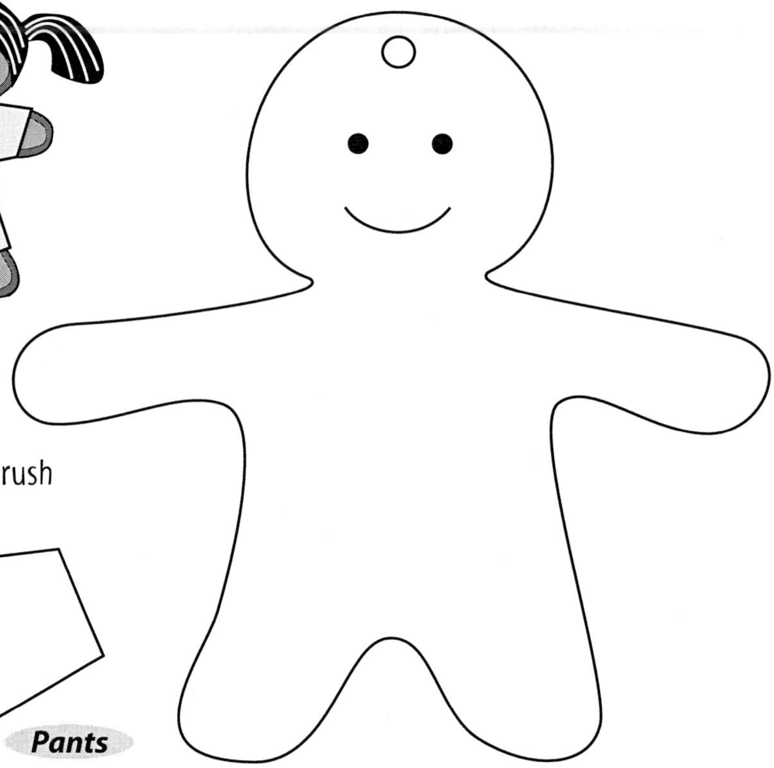

Materials (makes six)

- 1/4 cup applesauce
- 1/2 cup ground cinnamon
- caraway seeds, whole cloves
- 6 squares (3"), printed cotton fabric
- 3 yards, 1/8" satin ribbon
- Off-white and black acrylic paints, fine paintbrush
- 1 1/2 yards yarn
- white craft glue
- scissors
- paper towels

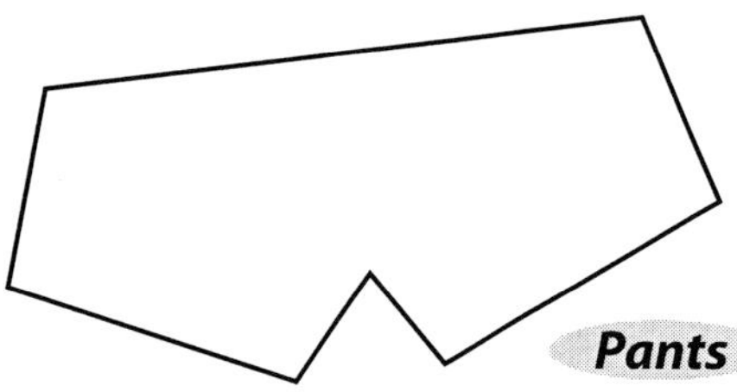

Pants

Directions

1. Trace clothing and body patterns onto poster board and cut them out. Cut the ribbon into 12" lengths
2. Gradually mix applesauce with 1/4 cup cinnamon in bowl. Add more cinnamon to make a dough and knead lightly. Sprinkle cinnamon on a cutting board and roll dough until it is 1/4" thin.
3. Use body pattern to cut out children. A straw can easily cut a hole in the top center of the head, to hang the ornament. Move the children to a flat surface covered with paper towels; let them dry for 24 hours.
4. Use the clothing patterns to cut dresses, shirts, and pants for the children. Glue clothing to the body. Cut 3" lengths of ribbon to make bows and glue them under the girls' chins. Glue tiny beads to the boy's shirt for buttons.
5. Draw eyes and mouths with the black and white paints.
6. Loop the 12" ribbon lengths through the head holes and knot tightly. Glue extra yarn for girls' hair and seeds for boys' hair.

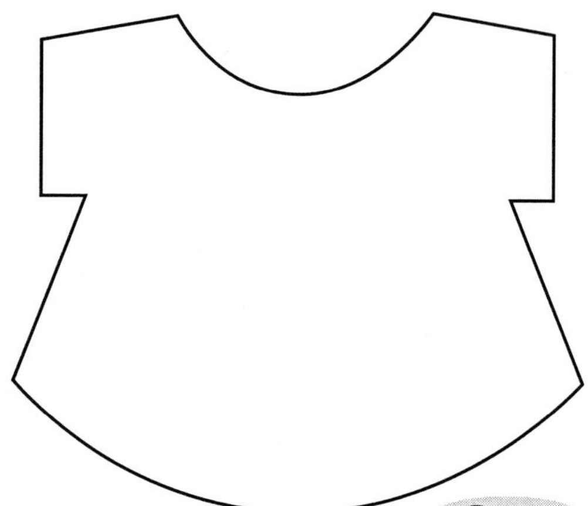

Dress

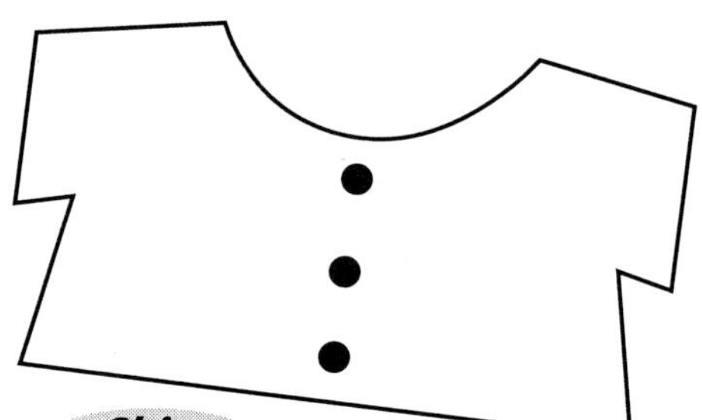

Shirt

Traditions! Traditions!

Which traditions does your family observe at Christmastime? Here are some ideas to try this season!

- Drive around to gaze at the colorful lights in your town on Christmas Eve.
- Ask your parents if your each member of the family can give one gift to someone else on Christmas Eve (note: everyone might not receive one, but the giving is what counts!).
- Encourage the guys to do the dishes on Christmas Day.
- Ask your mother or father to read the Christmas story to your family on Christmas Eve.
- Set all your stuffed animals and/or dolls under the tree until presents appear on Christmas morning.
- Count down the days till December 25th with an advent calendar.
- Learn some carols and sing them in your neighborhood some December evening. You might even get invited inside for cookies and hot cocoa!
- Assemble the other kids and whip up a special breakfast on Christmas morning for your parents!
- Ask your grandparents to tell stories from their childhood. Write them down so the next generations can treasure them as well.
- Gather new toys, new clothing, and non-perishable food items for a needy family. Place everything in a big basket, include some homemade cookies, and give it together as a family.
- Set aside a night to decorate and bake sugar cookies with your family.
- Recycle your Christmas tree at a park or wildlife area.
- Invite an international high school or college student to share Christmas with your family.
- Attend a midnight Christmas Eve service at a house of worship and sing old Christmas hymns.

Let It Snow...

How much do you know about snow? Find these snowy terms in the word search below. Note: terms with two words have no space between when found in the word search.

SNOW BANK

metamorphose (changing snow) ✲ **depth hoar** (large, cup-shaped crystals)
snowpack (depth of new and old snow) ✲ **needle ice** (forms in soil)
snow algae (plant growth beneath snow) ✲ **permafrost** (permanently frozen ground)
sugar snow (snow soft enough to burrow through) ✲ **spicule** (snow with ice protrusions)
glacier fire (highly reflective crusted ice) ✲ **hoar frost** (frozen dew)
firnification (thawing and re-freezing of snow) ✲ **wet snow** (snow containing water)
lenses (frozen layers of ice) ✲ **rime frost** (accumulated windblown snow on a surface)

```
F I R N I F I C A T I O N
X W Y E E B H G J S S I P
E E S E S N E L M N Q U E
S T G D E P T H H O A R R
O S X L G Z K I E W S L M
H N P E L T K L R A U G A
P O W I A Q J N A L G H F
R W I C C L R K W G A A R
O P K E I U W A S A R T O
M L P Y E B L B C E S S S
A U T G R W E E N K N P T
T S O R F R A O H H O Z R
E Y I H I Q Z N U T W I E
M J U T R K C A P W O N S
P R I M E F R O S T S N O
```

Merry Christmas!

Children around the world greet each other in different languages at Christmastime.
Practice saying a few of these foreign words that mean "Merry Christmas!"

Spanish Feliz Navidad
Norwegian God Jul
Portuguese Boas Festas
Turkish Noeliniz Ve Yeni Yiliniz Kutlu Olsun
Vietnamese Chung Mung Giang Sinh
French Joyeux Noel
Hindi Shub Naya Baras
Danish Glaedelig Jul
Korean Sung Tan Chuk Ha
Greek Kala Christouyenna
Italian Buone Feste Natalizie
Arabic Idah Saidan Wa Sanah Jadidah
Japanese Shinnen Omedeto
Thai Sawadee Pee Mai
Welsh Nadolig Llawen
Latin Natale Hilare
Polish Boze Narodzenie
Croatian Sretan Bozic
Hebrew Mo adim Lesimkha
Icelandic Gledileg Jol
German Froliche Weinachten

Quilting Bee

A quilt is one of the most special Christmas gifts of all. Quilts can tell a story, encourage friendship, express beauty, provide warmth, and show love.

Think about your favorite Christmas memories and illustrate them below in the nine quilt squares. Use the last square to draw a memory of this year's Christmas holiday!

Toasty Composing

In the United Kingdom, children eagerly wait for the arrival of Father Christmas each December. They write letters with their requests, just like American children. However, their lists aren't mailed to the North Pole. The children drop the letters into the fireplace instead! According to legend, the smoke from the letters rises through the chimney. Then Father Christmas reads the smoke!

Write a letter to Father Christmas. Tell him what you want for Christmas, why you want it, and why you should get it!

Old St. Nick

In the year 280 AD, a special boy was born in the present-day country of Turkey, which lies in Asia. Nicholas became a priest and then a bishop. He grew very wealthy, but he gave his money and other gifts to people all around the land. Nicholas didn't want attention or to be seen, so children were told to go to sleep quickly or he might not come! Many years after Nicholas died, the Eastern Catholic Church officially named Nicholas a saint for his good deeds and holy life. Stories of St. Nicholas spread around Europe and more than 2000 chapels and monasteries were named after him. St. Nicholas is still beloved by children all around the world today!

Match each "Santa Claus" with its country!

_____	Kris Kringle	A. Norway
_____	Ashenclos	B. Spain
_____	La Befana	C. Denmark
_____	Father Christmas	D. United States
_____	Saint Nicholas	E. Turkey
_____	Niklo	F. France
_____	Julenissen	G. China
_____	Sinter Klaas	H. England
_____	Pere Noel	I. Austria
_____	Julemanden	J. Germany
_____	Hotoeiosho	K. Russia
_____	Svaty Mikalas	L. Italy
_____	Dun Che Lao Ren	M. Holland
_____	Papa Noel	N. Czechoslovakia
_____	Babouschka	O. Sweden
_____	Jultomten	P. Japan

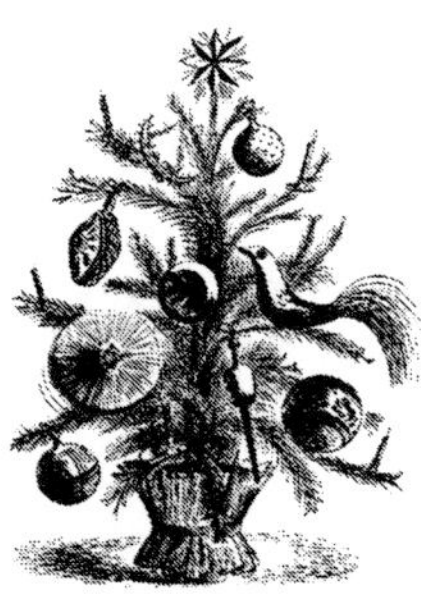

ANSWER KEY: D, J, L, H, E, I, A, M, F, C, P, N, G, B, K, O

Winter Wonderland!

Color the winter scene.

Holly Jolly Spelling Bee

Good spelling is a good habit! Study the words on the page. Most all of them can be found within the activities in this book! Then fold the right half of the page under. Take a "spelling test!" Ask a friend to read the words aloud to you. Write the correct spelling on the line. When finished, unfold the page and check your spelling. How many did you spell right? Study the words you miss.

WORDS

Christmas
reindeer
bell
Nativity
carol
rejoice
decorate
wreath
holiday
noel
present
celebrate
stocking
season
North Pole
mistletoe
solstice
sleigh
evergreen

Christmas Trivia

Unscramble the words below to discover some merry Christmas trivia!

WORD BANK

peace elves White billion
December female joy

1. Children in Italy used to hear stories about La Befana, a MEFELA __________ Santa Claus!

2. The best-selling Christmas single of all time is Bing Crosby's "HTWIE __________ Christmas."

3. In 2003, the United States Post Office will print more than four LLIBONI __________ postage stamps for Christmas.

4. Mistletoe is a symbol for PCEEA __________ and YJO ________.

5. According to legend, many LVESE __________ help Santa make toys for the good children around the world.

6. About 86% of consumers waits until DCEEEBMR __________ to do their Christmas shopping.

ANSWER KEY: 1-female, 2-White, 3-billion, 4-peace/joy, 5-elves, 6-December

Tra-la-la! Tra-la-la! Tra-la-la!

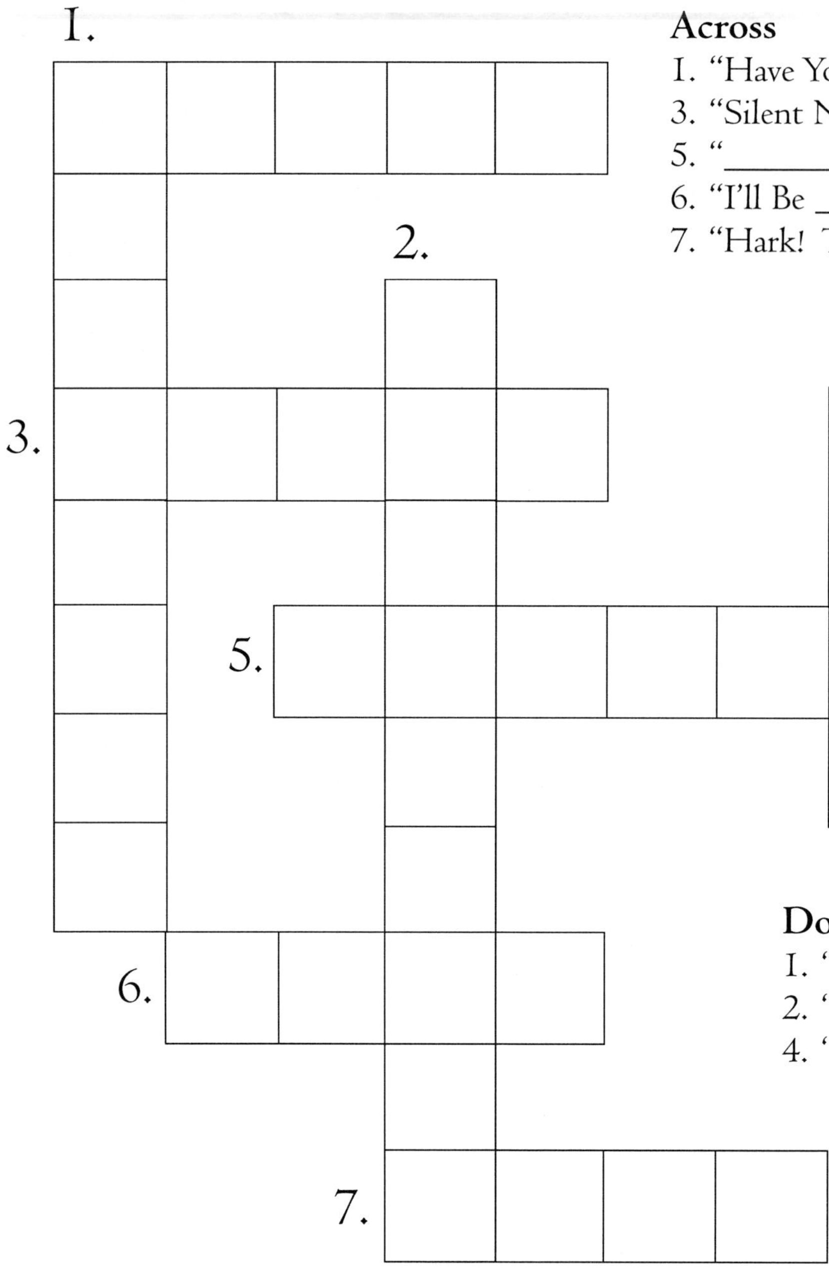

Across

1. "Have Yourself A ________ Little Christmas"
3. "Silent Night, Holy ____________"
5. "__________ Bells"
6. "I'll Be ______ For Christmas"
7. "Hark! The Herald Angels ________"

Down

1. "It Came Upon a __________ Clear"
2. "White ____________"
4. "The First __________"

Fast Fact!

"Silent Night, Holy Night" is sung in more than 180 languages around the world at Christmastime!

ANSWER KEY: (Across) 1-Merry, 3-Night, 5-Jingle, 6-Home, 7-Sing; (Down) 1-Midnight, 2-Christmas, 4-Noel

What Does It All Mean, Anyway?

Most folks agree that Christmas is a wonderful and special holiday, but not everyone feels the same about what it means. Many families think Christmas is a time to be with relatives and enjoy old traditions. Some people celebrate the birth of Christ and love to sing old hymns. Others just enjoy the peaceful time of year and remember to be thankful for their many blessings.

What does Christmas mean to you? Write your response in a descriptive paragraph below. (Hint: there are no wrong answers!)

Merry Christmas!

Acrostic poems are composed by writing a word or phrase that starts with each letter of a word. Next to every letter, write a word or phrase about Christmas. The first letter is done for you. Now let's see what you can do!

C hestnuts roasting on an open fire!

H ______________________________

R ______________________________

I ______________________________

S ______________________________

T ______________________________

M ______________________________

A ______________________________

S ______________________________